If It Fits, I Sits

If It Fits, I Sits

Cats in Awkward Places

First published in Great Britain
in 2015 by Orion

10 9 8 7 6 5 4 3

A CIP catalogue record for this book is
available from the British Library.

ISBN: 978 1409 16073 1

Edited by Holly Harley
Designed by Goldust Design
Printed in Italy

MIX
Papier aus verantwor-
tungsvollen Quellen
FSC® C023419
www.fsc.org

The Orion Publishing Group Ltd
Carmelite House
50 Victoria Embankment
London EC4Y 0DZ

An Hachette UK Company

www.orionbooks.co.uk

This is just my resting face.

Why do you keep so much money and food down here?!

Why can't cats hibernate? I need to hibernate right here.

These boots were made for snuggling, actually.

You have no idea what kind of day I've had.

I didn't choose the flop life – the flop life chose me.

If you insist on putting treats in weird places, don't be surprised about finding me in weird places.

I'm not sure how this happened but please just help.

Gardening is so much effort anyway.

You wouldn't know, but the waffle fur effect is so hot right now.

Have you tried turning it off and on again?

Let's be honest – cats are far more your bag.

I'm auditioning for a *National Geographic* cover.

You're terribly grouchy without coffee.

This is the only time your socks are approachable, so I'm making the most of it.

I'm the slickest Jedi you've ever seen.

How am I going to get out of here with no curtains to climb up?

You don't need to open the blinds. You have me to look at.

File me under 'S' for sleeping.

You don't need
this right?

Too-small boxes are the best kind of boxes.

Just hold me.

So... someone ate your lunch.

Yeah, I can see your problem back here – loads of cat hair everywhere.

If I'm not supposed to sit here then why is it so warm?

Ah, you're here! Turn on the tap, I need a drink.

You have so many handbags, why do you need this one right now?

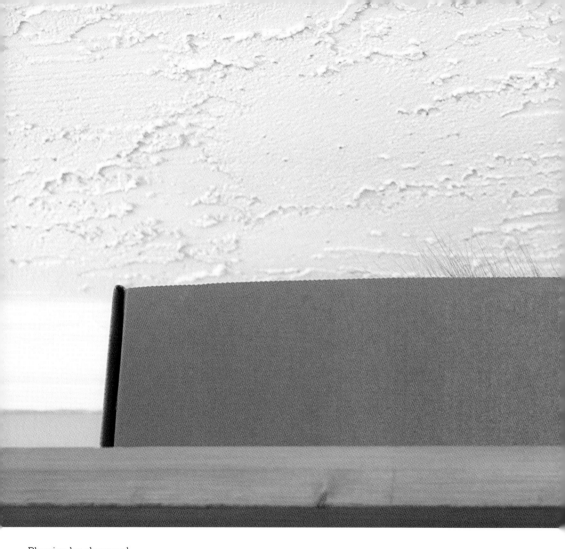

Physics be damned.

Can you explain why it's bad to be in the gutter? We love it here.

Stop feeding the birds and feed me.

What do you mean 'this isn't your new scratching post'?

Oh, hi.

A tyre swing? Don't be ridiculous. It's much better like this.

What's 'tetanus'?

You... might need to run this again.

Living on the edge is exhausting.

Perfect.

Let's save you some of the pain: yeah, you're broke.

Just leave me for a bit. I need time to get over the sight of that number on the scales...

Take this thing off the hook and cuddle me.

Have I created my own force field?!

This better not go the same way it did for the itsy bitsy spider.

It's so far to the ground!

Well, being a tightrope
walker myself...

Where are you going?
Take me with you.

Printer jam? Nope, nothing wrong here.

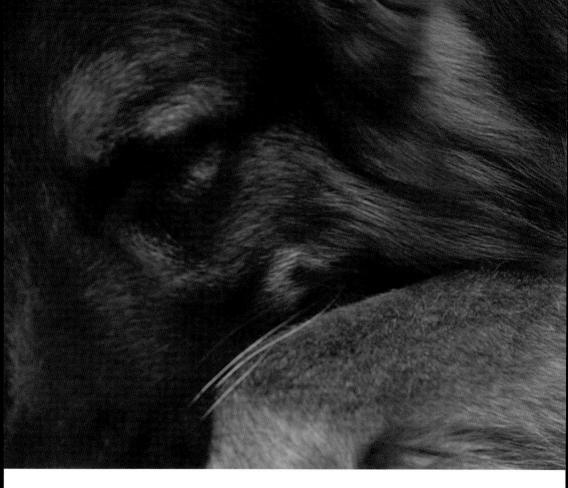

You may be man's best friend, dog, but you're my best place to sit.

Does this make me Cinderella?

Why would you photograph this? The bag clashes horribly with our fur.

I have no idea where I am… but it's warm, so it'll do.

Are you implying I'm too large for one chair?

All will be well once my body is at exactly ninety degrees.

Look me in the eyes and try to move me. I know I'm too cute to be moved.

Towels are always better with a bit of fluff on.

What? You need to put water in here? But I'm in here!

Hello there.

I still fit.

As comfy as ever.

I woke up like this.

I don't care if you need this hat, I'm never leaving.

Hurry up and hang the decorations so I can biff them down again.

Can I help you?

Maybe if we snuggle tightly enough we'll become one giant cat...

It's not very airy in here, but it'll do.

Why are there so many things in your handbag but never any treats?!

I can tell you're jealous that I never get that wicker stripe on my bottom.

I'll admit the creaking sounds are worrying me.

Best sunbathing spot ever!

You get on with the papers – I'll take care of the important business.

I've been to better spas, to be honest.

What? 'Some assembly required'? No. Shut up.

Some of these look a bit dirty... don't worry, I'll clean them.

Your alphabetisation skills leave much to be desired.

Believe it or not, I planned this.

Let me check your schedule: yeah, it's back-to-back tickles under the chin with me all afternoon.

Why can't you bring something exciting back in these bags for once, like ham?

I should feel no shame for being here! I see you sneaking in here at night!

Come at me, winter.

I don't have to explain anything to you.

If I keep still enough, I might win the birds' trust...

I dream of being so fluffy I fill this bag.

Yes, I'm going to lie here like this if you don't leave my boxes open for me.

I tried to sit... something went wrong.

I hope I can rely on you to catch me if I start to slip.

Where was this when I got stuck in that tree all afternoon?!

I'm so much prettier than your fruit.

Backpacking is awesome.

Chill. Your plants will be fine.

I'll try to not snag all your tights with my claws but I can't promise anything.

This is a fine chariot. For once, you have done well.

I like the classics most. You can really immerse yourself in them.

Let's face it... you're never going to read all of these.

Hey! Need a bookmark?

Let me know when's best to for me to come down there with my dusty feet.

Did you just say 'hubcats'? Oh, wow.

I'd destroy you in a limbo competition.

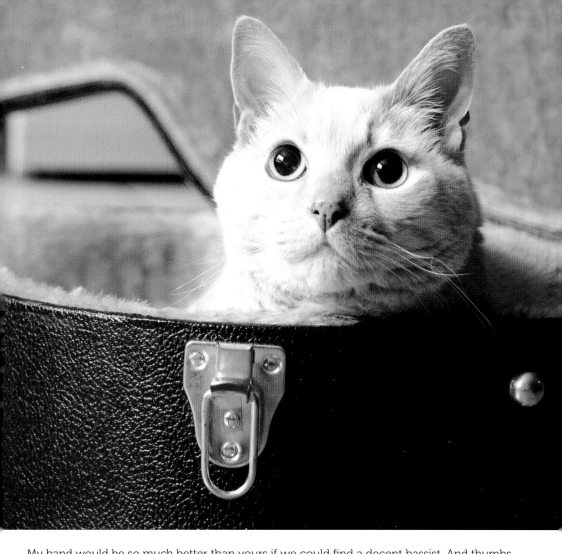

My band would be so much better than yours if we could find a decent bassist. And thumbs.

Worship me.

Don't even try to come near me with things to put in this bowl.

The comfort of being here only just outweighs the smell.

Just tell me where the treats are.

Well, I just about fit...

If I promise to leave the curtains intact can I stay up here...?

Soon, human.

Check out my ride.

I'm getting more satisfaction out of this new thing for the kitchen than you ever will.

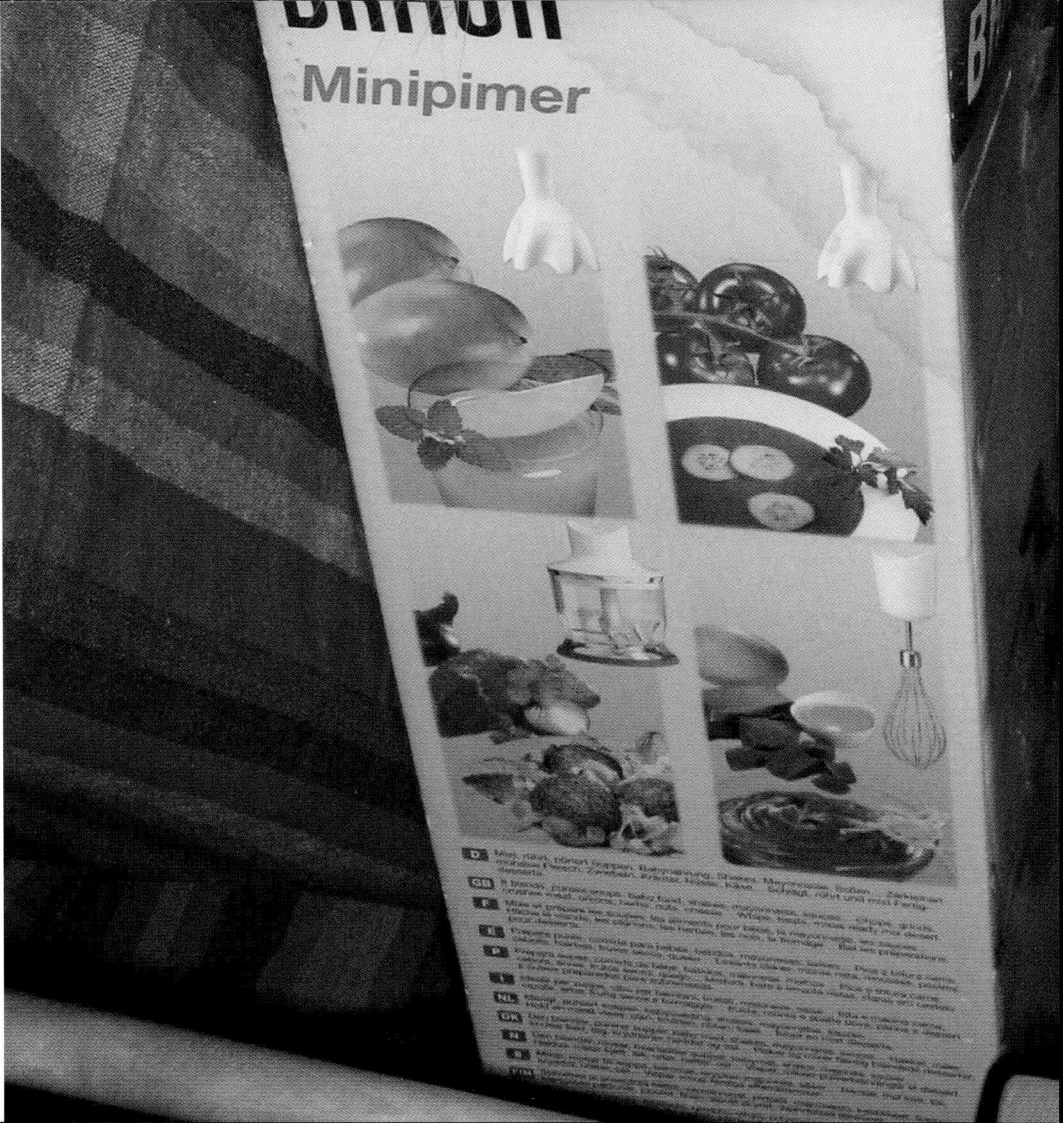
Minipimer

I'm happy... just not sure how I'll get down.

This invention is genius.

Nice of you to drop by!

I will not rest until I am perfectly circular.

I can be flat, so I fit. What's the problem?

The secret to comfort actually
lies in this outstretched paw.

Someone's been
scratching the DVDs?!

MYPROTEIN™
FUEL YOUR AMBITION

You're going to need a lot more than just ambition.

Might need a hand getting out of here... might stay here for the next three hours. Not sure yet.

I'm pretty sure if I can get through here I could escape prison.

You don't want to know what I'm doing in here.

The best thing about plastic crates is this little bit where I can rest a tiny part of my face.

Another shopping trip, still no ham. I'm not angry, I'm just disappointed.

I know it's only been six seconds but can I come back inside?

'Use it as a toboggan,' they said, 'we'll come get you,' they said...

Forget your nativity.
I'm the star.

If you could just keep
getting bigger shoes as
I grow that'd be great.

I think I've forgotten which limb is which.

Sorry, no room here. You're going to have to take the floor.

Picture credits

DaLy/Shutterstock

Wilson Pickett
Emily Smith

*Maurizio Cefano/
19Cefa94/Flickr/
Creative Commons*

Loki
Rebekah Davies

Lena Lir/Shutterstock

*Agata Dorobek/
Shutterstock*

Eric Cantona
Adele Pullarp

Maksymowicz/iStock

Boris
Henry Hemming

*ivanoffotography/
Shutterstock*

fzd.it/Shutterstock

BettinaSampl/iStock

apolonia/Shutterstock

Caxton
Chris Stork

The Len/Shutterstock

Hanzi-mor/
Shutterstock

Sari O'Neal/
Shutterstock

valiooo/iStock

anurakpong/iStock

MaxyM/Shutterstock

Renata Osinska/
Shutterstock

Valeri Potapova/
Shutterstock

ferrerivideo/iStock

ahloch/iStock

uccia_photography/
Getty

Benoit Daoust/
Shutterstock

Eugenio Marongiu/
Shutterstock

Belle
BoulderPhoto/Shutterstock

Bezzangi/Shutterstock

bigworld/iStock

In Tune/Shutterstock

ian35mm/iStock

volcank/iStock

OndagoArts/iStock

Aubord Dulac/
Shutterstock

DeltaOFF/iStock

BettinaSampl/iStock

Zanna Holstova/
Shutterstock

Nataliya Kuznetsova/
Shutterstock

Avangard Photography/
Shutterstock

PawelG Photo/
Shutterstock

Anna Jurkovska/
Shutterstock

apeyron/Shutterstock

Pidgoma Levgeniia/
Shutterstock

mzamur/iStock

Malibu
Giuliana Heatherington

Malibu
Giuliana Heatherington

Gato
Mercedes Basso

Valentina Razumova/
Shutterstock

Bela
Duncan Millar &
Francisco Oliveira

Zanna Holstova/
Shutterstock

Edinorog/iStock

Fannie/Autumn Barnes/
autbarnes08/Flickr/
Creative Coimmons

mugensx/iStock

Andrey_Kuzmin/
Shutterstock

MaxyM/Shutterstock

EMstudio/Shutterstock

Sylvia sooyoN/
Shutterstock

Herbie
Cathryn Gilbert

Frankieleon/Flickr/
Creative Commons

Rappholdt/Shutterstock

fotata/Shutterstock

ivz/iStock

Joanna Zaleska/iStock

FooTToo/iStock

Nadinelle/Shutterstock

Pebbles
Alex Pidduck

John Ruskin
Marta Owczarek

Kichigin/Shutterstock

olcha/Shutterstock

Brutus
Annie Martin

Claude
Kimberly Washford

DreamBig/Shutterstock

Zanna Holstova/
Shutterstock

Marlinde/Shutterstock

Manja/Shutterstock

Gail Johnson/
Shutterstock

horvathta/Shutterstock

IrinaK/Shutterstock

Koldunov Alexey/
Shutterstock

Mac99/iStock

cip1000/iStock

Ben
Pat Bland

Lovely
Lisa Milton

wideshuts/Shutterstock

liveostockimages/
iStock

Tinks
Rebecca Sharman

wolfman57/
Shutterstock

dogi/Shutterstock

Photoseeker/
Shutterstock

Francesca Yorke/Getty

Steve
CaptMikey9/Flickr/
Creative Commons

Phooey/iStock

Charlie
David Bamford

DaLy/Shutterstock

Nutmeg
Lucie Stericker

epicurean/iStock

NicO_l/Shutterstock

mariakbell/iStock

fiorigianluigi/iStock

*ThomasShanahan/
iStock*

Evgeny Sergeev/iStock

*Benoit Daoust/
Shutterstock*

Nadinelle/Shutterstock

Viesinsh/iStock

John Ruskin
Marta Owczarek

*Anna Jurkovska/
Shutterstock*

Mouse
Suzie Doore

Neil
Sebastian Rydberg

*Daniel Gale/
Shutterstock*

Sitikka/iStock

soulrebel83/iStock

ferrerivideo/iStock

Meoita/Shutterstock

Waffle
Amanda Jones

Smokey Joe
Anna Valentine

Vampirica/iStock

mrak_hr/iStock

Vampirica/iStock

paranoix/iStock

Max
Judy Gee

Karl Umbriaco/
Shutterstock

vvvita/iStock

Jesus Christ
Natasha Vouckelatou

Belle
Amanda Thursby

Zhenikeyev/iStock

Monty
Charlotte Morris